# OVERCOMING
## THE ADDICTION
## THAT NO ONE HAS

# OVERCOMING
## THE ADDICTION
## THAT NO ONE HAS

ANDREW J. LANDRY

The Author's Pen, LLC

USA

**The Author's Pen, LLC**
**PO Box 720798**
**Houston, Texas 77272**
**www.tapwriting.com**

Scripture quotations, unless otherwise noted, are taken from the NEW KING JAMES (NKJV) of the Bible. Copyright© 1979 1980, 1982, by Thomas Nelson, Inc., publishers.

Disclaimer: This book is based on real life experiences. However, some names, identities, and circumstances are changed in order to protect the integrity and anonymity of the individuals involved. Anyone experiencing issues with addiction of any sort, please seek professional help. This book is not meant to cure addiction, it is a testimony of how the author managed to *Overcome the Addiction that No One Has*.

**Overcoming the Addiction that No One Has, Andrew J. Landry**. -- 1st Print ed.
ISBN 978-1-948248-02-0

# Dedication

This book is dedicated to my mother Kathy Jones, who taught me to be responsible for my actions. You have always stressed the importance of doing the right thing even when it's hard.

To all the individuals *Overcoming the Addiction that No One Has*, remember, you are not alone.

# Special Thanks

A very special thank you to Pastor Ronald Eagleton, Korey Eagleton, Amber LaTrece, Kathy Jones, Ashley Landry (Collier), Andrew J Landry II, Tre' J. Landry, and my wife, Katrina M. Landry. Your support during this process and throughout life, means more than you know.

# CONTENTS

# INTRODUCTION: THE MAKING OF A SEX ADDICT

At one point, I was happily married with children, had a successful career, and the picture-perfect life. I had arrived, my life was together, or at least that's how it seemed. Who would have thought I would go from my perfect little scenario – to sitting in my car, bankrupt with a house in foreclosure? I didn't see it coming, but that too was part of my perfect scenario. I never thought too long or hard about how my decisions would impact the people I love or the life I enjoyed. I lost everything, all because of this thing called addiction.

Funny thing, I always thought addiction was limited to drugs and alcohol, but I struggled with neither, sex had a hold on me. *I was a sex addict.*

For as long as I can remember, sex has been part of my life, and to some degree, I became desensitized to normal affection. It wasn't what I planned; the flame grew into a full blaze and had overtaken me and everything in its path. The voice of addiction became louder than reason and clouded my vision to the point hurting the very people I love.

After being violated at a young age, spending years of my life confused, and having a dysfunctional idea of intimacy; the addiction brought me full circle to face the truth about the man I had become. It forced me into a decision. I had to decide who I wanted to be and how I wanted to love.

In this book, I will take you on a journey through my personal struggles, some of the lessons I've learned, but more importantly, the steps I took to overcome. My hope is to start a conversation around sexual addiction, to be a voice that speaks truth and facilitates freedom from the prison of our shameful pasts. I know what it is to suffer in silence and want to empower you to make a different choice.

As I look back on the day I sat homeless and bankrupt, I couldn't help but wonder…What will be greater than my addiction? That thought would later prove to be the rudder, or steering mechanism of my life. It is my hope that through my story you too will find the thing to steer your life as you transition from private pain and secret struggle to a place of victory.

# CHAPTER ONE

# UNDERSTANDING SEX ADDICTION

Whether this book was given to you as a gift or if you grabbed a copy for yourself, you need some understanding of sexual addiction. Like many people, I never thought of sex as something a person could be addicted to because it's a natural part of life. Educating ourselves about this addiction brings more awareness. Although we all have personal experiences, here's where we'll take a more general look at sex addiction.

## What is sexual addiction?

Sexual addiction falls under the scope of compulsive sexual behavior. According to a 2015 article by Katherine L. Derbyshire, Department of Psychiatry & Behavioral Neuroscience, University of Chicago,

"Compulsive sexual behavior (CSB) is a common disorder featuring repetitive, intrusive and distressing sexual thoughts, urges and behaviors that negatively affect many aspects of an individual's life. Compulsive sexual behavior can generally be divided into two categories: Paraphilic and nonparaphilic.

Nonparaphilic CSB, which is characterized by more typical sexual desires, include compulsive sexual acts with multiple partners, constant fixation on a partner that may be considered unobtainable, compulsive masturbation, compulsive use of pornography, and compulsive sex and sexual acts within a consensual relationship." *

You'll notice, I want to focus our attention on Nonparaphilic because that was my experience. My desires were typical, all consensual and somewhat socially acceptable, which masked the addiction.

An earlier source, Dr. Timothy Fong, Assistant Clinical Professor of Psychiatry and Director of UCLA Impulse Control Disorders Clinic reports in a 2006 article,

"Compulsive sexual behavior, otherwise known as sexual addiction, is an emerging psychiatric disorder that has significant medical and psychiatric consequences. Until recently, very little empirical data existed to explain the biological, psychological, and

5

social risk factors that contribute to this condition. In addition, clinical issues, such as the natural course and best practices on treating sexual addictions, have not been formalized. Despite this absence, the number of patients and communities requesting assistance with this problem remains significant." *

## Who struggles with sexual addiction?

Although some women struggle with sexual addiction, it's more common for men. That's a major reason why I decided to write this book. Let's talk about what we're going through, heal ourselves, and get on with the business of life.

According to a 2013 Time Magazine article which highlighted findings from a study Sex Addiction: A Disease or a Convenient Excuse,

> "Sex addiction may threaten health and social relationships: 28% of those diagnosed contracted an STD at least once, 39% had lost relationships and 17% had lost jobs because of their condition.

> The findings also highlighted intriguing gender divides among sufferers: 95% of those seeking help for sexual compulsion at one of the study treatment centers were male but 40% of those diagnosed at psychiatric and addiction centers were women,

suggesting that although the disorder may genuinely be more common in men, women may be less likely to seek help for it.

And contrary to popular portrayals of sex addicts as spending their nights having intercourse with multiple partners, the vast majority of the compulsive sexual behavior among those diagnosed with disorder in the study involved masturbation and pornography. Over three quarters of participants reported problems with pornography, but only 45% engaged in compulsive sex with other consenting adults and 45% cheated on their primary partners. Those who did have partnered sex averaged 15 sexual partners in the past year." *

Sharing statistics is my way of informing you that sex addiction isn't uncommon. There are people struggling in private.

Based on my experience, there are distinct characteristics of a sex addict. Sex becomes associated with your identity, you base your self-worth on how much sex you're having and how good at it you are. When you feel deprived of sex, the addiction can cause other bad habits to manifest. This rang especially true for me during my high school years.

In the coming chapters, I will share personal accounts of how I struggled, stages of how addiction claimed years of my life, and the victory I now enjoy because I had the courage to change. I want you to see yourself somewhere in these pages and understand you're not alone. I want you to walk away believing you too can consciously and intentionally experience the liberty of creating the life you want with the people you love.

# CHAPTER TWO

# SUFFERING IN SILENCE

Now that we have a better understanding of sexual addiction, I'd like to share my story. It's one thing to suffer but another to suffer in silence. Keeping quiet keeps you in the posture of suffering and a place where you can't get help from others. And understand, sex addiction is a lonely, conflict-ridden experience.

## Why I Remained Silent?

On one hand, sex is natural and normal. On the other, it's shameful and embarrassing. Physical intimacy is how humans interact, right? In a committed, responsible relationship like marriage there's not a second thought about sex. It's a given. It's how we reproduce and keep this thing called life happening. But, there's an extreme, dysfunctional side when it's experienced with compulsion; the place where shame showed up.

According to a 2016 article Characteristics of self-identified sexual addicts in a behavioral addiction outpatient clinic, "Sexual addiction has also been linked to sexual abuse during childhood and has been associated with a variety of unhealthy and risky behaviors, including risky sexual practices."

*

There are analysts who believe sexual abuse during childhood can trigger a life of sex addiction. That idea seemed a little too easy for me, but maybe on a subconscious level, this has something to do how things unfolded in my life. I'm not a psychiatrist and don't pretend to be. I blame my abusers for teaching me a behavior that would not only negatively impact my life but also the lives of many others.

**Where it Began**

It was late September or early October. I walked in the room and sat in front of the TV. I don't remember what was on, but whatever it was I didn't watch it for long. From the doorway, she watched me. After a moment, she called me to the restroom. I thought nothing of this since she was an older woman and a good friend of my mother's. I'd been in proximity to her before. My mother visited her frequently, sometimes bringing my sister and I along. We'd play at their feet while they talked about the Bible passages, what Sister so-and-so wore to Bible study, or just life in general. Our families were close. I can remember hanging out with them and having fellowship.

This day marked a new experience for me. She pulled me into the bathroom, shut and locked the door behind her. I turned to look at it, but she knelt to the floor in front of me, her hands around my wrists as she smiled maternally. Next, she took off my clothes, slowly peeled back layers until only my body was exposed. I felt shy, but she only smiled again. She took off her own clothes and laid down on the cold floor. She urged me to bend down and took my hand again. Then she stroked me with her hands. I think I was excited when she put me inside of her.

As I look back, what confused me most was she was so much older and more experienced than I was, yet she still thought I could satisfy her. I didn't have a clue about how to satisfy her or fulfill her needs. I didn't even know what her needs were. This was my first experience. While I had no say so in it, it started a trend for me. I can't remember how many times the abuse happened, but the only people who ever knew our secret were she and I. She always told me not to tell, but I'm certain she knew she never had to worry about this. I couldn't tell my mother for obvious reasons. Since I was only three-years-old, I didn't have any friends or acquaintances to talk to. As a result, this became a normal way of life for me, and our secret continued for years.

11

Fast forward about three years, and things became more complicated. A different culprit preyed upon me. With years of experience under my belt, I was a little more up to speed on how these situations worked. I was groomed well enough to believe this was natural. The scenario was similar. This new person was also close to my mother and someone she sat and talked to on numerous occasions. This person was family. Naturally, it was a familiar place for me to find myself in.

Unlike the times before, this culprit was a guy. His approach was starkly different. Where the former had failed to teach me, he showed me the ropes. Now he was trying to enter me like she encouraged me to do to her. For some reason unbeknownst to me then, it never worked quite how he wanted it to. Each time we would see each other, we would continue in our endeavors. As time passed, I participated more willingly, learning I could do the same things he did. He was teaching me how to be a man, giving me clues, mannerisms, and experience with how to properly handle these encounters. This occurred when I was around six-years-old but continued for about ten more years.

By the time I turned sixteen, I was molested for thirteen years of my life. In some way, I believed it was normal. My silence began before I understood what being silent was.

Keeping secrets contributed to being victimized.

> According to a 2014 article An Epidemiological
> Overview of Child Sexual Abuse (CSA), "This si-
> lence is due to the fear of indignity, denial from the
> community, social stigma, not being able to trust gov-
> ernment bodies, and gap in communication between
> parents and children about this issue." *

The cycle of suffering continued because of my silence.

# CHAPTER THREE

# TEENAGE YEARS

High school was an interesting time. As for most adolescent, I went through my coming of age experience and had to contend with raging hormones. Looking back, I see how I continued the same old pattern.

While I had a natural ability in sports and never felt inadequate in that area, sex proved more rewarding. There were flings. I had a brief encounter with one of my sister's friends and another older girl but still I had gained little of a reputation. Fulfilling my desires seemed difficult. I knew I had to push myself out my comfort zone. A lot of my friends partied, so I followed suit and sneaked out to drink. Many nights, I was so drunk my friends had to help me back into my bedroom window. Those nights became more frequent, serving as a venue for my sexual encounters. As mentioned, I was an athlete in school. This meant I was popular by default.

By high school, I developed many relationships. I was never the arrogant or obnoxious type, so people enjoyed being around me. I made friends with most of my basketball, football and tennis teammates. I enjoyed being around my female friends but maintaining true relationships with them was difficult, since I constantly thought about having sex with them. It did not matter their size, shape, color, or background. Sex was what I knew best, and it was important to have as much of it as I could.

During the later months of my sophomore year, I finally met a girl. She was a nice young lady, and we were interested in each other. We courted, and it wasn't long before I displayed how knowledgeable I was about sex. I saw her every day at school and spent almost every night at her house. We had sex almost daily. I still don't know how others found out about this, but soon the word was out. I thought others wanted to experience what we had, and I soon had sex with other people in our circle. In my opinion, sex was supposed to be shared with those closest to you. Being from a small town, we were close with all the same people. This was fine with me and felt normal. My abusers were all close to me.

On some level, I felt like I was given a gift, and I wanted to share it with as many people as possible. I assumed I was more experienced than the other guys in our school. After all, my history went back a lot farther than theirs.

# CHAPTER FOUR

# BEFORE I KNEW I HAD A PROBLEM

I was just a kid when I entered my first marriage. Looking back, I wasn't ready for the responsibility of monogamy, so naturally I stepped outside of the marriage.

She was an attractive older woman who had her own car and job. She was in college, and more experienced than the high school girls I previously dated. We connected on a deeper sexual level than I could with them. By the time things started to taper off with her, graduation was upon me. I walked across the stage feeling accomplished. I was beyond ready to start real life and abandon high school drama and girls. Little did I know; high school drama was nothing compared to the whirlwind I was about to be thrown into.

My addiction had real consequences. She called me late one night crying hysterically. When I finally calmed her down enough to understand why she was crying, I soon felt the same panic. She was pregnant. Since I couldn't process the news, I didn't tell anyone for a couple of days. Coming from one of the last generations of do the right thing, I knew I needed to marry her. Running from the responsibility never crossed my mind. She came home from school, had our baby, and married me as planned, even though I'm not sure she wanted to at the time.

Married life was strange and came in stark contrast to the life I was accustomed to. My youth and immaturity contrasted with her feistiness and high education. There wasn't a day we didn't fight about something. I've never been keen on conflict. When the fight would get too intense, I would run away from it and her.

My father was never around as I grew up, and this drove my desire to be a model father for my daughter. Even though I ran from conflict, I never ran from the relationship. Amid all the fighting, arguing, and drama, I stuck around. I was determined to give my daughter a life with two married parents who loved her even if they didn't like each other. To give my daughter the childhood that I was robbed of, I took her everywhere with me, even to the gym. She was the epitome of daddy's little girl.

While I constantly focused on being a good dad, I never considered being a good husband a priority. I wanted nothing to do with my wife. The incessant fighting was too much and caused me to grow cold in the relationship. Feeling unaccomplished caused me to fall back into old habits easily. My insecurity made me go outside of my marriage for gratification. This was comfortable, familiar, and allowed me to avoid making any other commitments I wasn't ready to keep. In addition, I didn't have to leave my marriage, or be miserable either. It seemed better this way, at least that's what I told myself.

Eventually, she found out about my infidelity. I was lazy about covering my tracks and didn't regret cheating. When she decided to divorce me, I wasn't upset. Subconsciously, I checked out a long time ago and ended up dating the married woman who I cheated on her with. Her, her husband and I played softball together. We planned our escapades. It was an avenue to cope with the conflict and drama I was experiencing at home.

I hung out at their house, played with their kids, and had sex with her in their home without him becoming suspicious or ever finding out. Their marriage eventually ended. After it dissolved, I lived with her for a little more than a year. I enjoyed her company. Still, I was not being completely fulfilled in my sexual endeavors. It's not because she wasn't giving it to me, but because I became greedy. Like I did to women before her, I had sex with some of her close friends. Even after all I went through, I couldn't help but feel that sex was reserved for those closest to a person. Eventually growing tired of pretending, I became distant.

This was the first time I felt disturbed. I can remember being nervous about getting caught. The meetings became more frequent and easier, and we took calculated risks. It was mentally challenging having to make sure every base was covered. At the time, the risk was worth the reward. I was a slave to my vices back then. Keep in mind, this was before I knew I had a problem and before I sought treatment.

# CHAPTER FIVE

# BACHELOR SEASON

After coming off the heels of a divorce and subsequent failed relationships, I knew I needed a change. At the same time, I knew I wasn't ready to change. My friends suggested I be single, then I would be free to do as I pleased and not have to drag anyone along with me.

I rejected that idea. Relationships, especially sexual ones, were enhanced by being close to someone, and I wanted that. As the seeds of change began to sprout, the sexual aspect of my life diminished.

I began dating a young lady, she and I seemed to have everything intact. I figured this time I would not rush into having sex. I realized what I had been doing, wasn't working. I wanted to change, not only for me, but I could see the hurt I caused in the lives of people I cared for or thought I cared about. We dated for a couple of years and it happened; I cheated. This time with someone familiar. Familiarity has a way of breeding closeness.

I remained single but continued to be sexually active with many others. This was one of the best and worst times in my life, and one of the loneliest. When hookups were scarce, I threw myself into work and sports, but there was rarely a shortage of partners. Sometimes I wanted more, but whenever I thought about my history, I knew I wasn't ready. I lied to many people, but more than anything I was tired of lying to myself.

One of those partners was the ex-wife who I cheated on. At the time she wasn't dating anyone, so she and I rekindled the old flame. I was excited because I would be with my daughter again. Being a good father was still my goal. We began our life together again. We bought a car and a house together. At the time I was selling cars, so I was making good money and could take care of us. Although she was still more educated, I was in a better place. I was more mature and prepared compared to when I was fresh out of high school. My life experiences rivaled hers now, and she no longer seemed more experienced with the ways of the world. We were back on the path to forever, and I'd be lying if I said it didn't feel good.

But, like many times before, I fell back into the pattern I called life. I grew tired with what seemed good and drifted into something else which wouldn't last.

After my season of so-called-singleness, I went back to another familiar relationship. I couldn't imagine myself happy without companionship.

# CHAPTER SIX

# WHAT'S DONE IN THE DARK MUST COME TO THE LIGHT

Marriage was the furthest thing from my mind. With one marriage under my belt, I wasn't looking for a second one. However, a second marriage found me.

## A New Love Interest

I felt a sense of danger the moment one of my sisters brought a referral to the dealership. When I saw them pull up in my sister's car that Friday evening, I couldn't help but to curse myself and think God was taunting me. I was stationed near the door, like we were trained to do. My sister stepped through first, hugging me as she turned to look at her friend dressed in jeans and blouse.

"Andrew, this is the friend I told you about. She's been look-ing for a new car, and I thought you might be able to help her out."

"I can certainly try," I said. With a smile on my face, I shook her hand, which was soft and slightly damp from the heat outside. I asked her the usual questions. Car or truck? Se-dan or coupe? Any color preferences or amenities? How far do you normally commute from work to home? Do you prefer to buy new or used? I quickly got a clear idea of what she wanted. She was flexible for the most part, but my ex-wife and I had plans to go to a wake that evening for one of my friends. So, I asked if she could come back Saturday morning.

She showed up in a black and white Adidas jumpsuit. Her time was limited because she had other plans. We looked at a few cars, drove a few, and narrowed down to what worked. The perfect car for her was being used by one of our other customers and would not be back until late that Saturday evening. Because she let me know she wouldn't be available the rest of the day, I asked her to come that Sunday. The deal-ership was closed on Sundays. Since I had plans to go fishing with my homeboy Sunday morning, I asked her to meet me around 1 p.m.

After she left with my sister, I immediately exited the sales floor to look for my manager. I walked straight to his office and knocked on the black door frame before I entered. He stressed that he had an open-door policy, but I still felt like it was rude to barge in.

"What's up, Drew?"

"Hey, man. How's it going? I just wanted to ask you a quick question."

"Ask away," he said. To ensure I received his full attention, he closed the manila folder he was working from and locked his computer screen.

"I know we're not open tomorrow, but I have a client who I think will buy if we can schedule her a test drive tomorrow afternoon. She was in earlier, but she had a couple of things come up, so we weren't able to do it today. Would it be ok if I set it up?"

"Of course! No problem at all. Just let whoever is closing know, so you can get in."

"Awesome, thank you so much."

"Anything else," he asked.

"I'm going to marry that girl one day," I said.

"Boy, shut your ass up. You and your ex-wife just got back together, done got the house, and the car. Talking about marrying this girl. If you don't shut up."

"Yeah, yeah, I know. But I will marry her. Just wait and see."

We chuckled and went back out to the sales floor. I assured him I would definitely close this deal.

## The Following Day

I arrived at the dealership a few minutes before 1 p.m. She was already there, wearing a short sundress. I greeted her and told her to wait while I got the car she would eventually buy. As we were test driving, I noticed there was something special about her. She loved to smile and was very sexy. What I liked most was her flexibility. We were both in relationships, but I asked her to meet me for lunch the next day. Monday morning when I arrived to work, my manager asked me how the test drive went. I played it safe and told him it went well, adding that she would stop by later to sign paperwork.

I left all I re-established with my ex-wife. About one month later, we moved in together. My heart told me now was the time to work on making a forever for myself and this new love interest of mine. She was all I had, so I wanted it to work this time. I was getting desperate. The string of failed relationships was weighing heavily on me. Being a good father was still one of my top priorities. My goal was to set an example for my daughter of what a healthy relationship was. This was my opportunity to get it right with someone who loved me as much as I loved them. I waited until we were living together to have sex.

By this time, I gained at least a few degrees of what I called self-control, which I could use when necessary. I wanted more than anything to do right by her, and I thought we had a shot at making it work. She was more like me than the others were. This time, I wasn't the only one starting a relationship with another person. She cheated, too. We both knew what the other was capable of and vowed to be open and honest in our relationship.

Within a month of us living together, she was pregnant. This was fine by me. A few months later, we were married. My manager was more than congratulatory. For once, I felt accomplished. Here I was living the dream. I had a sexy and beautiful wife who I enjoyed spending my time with. She was about to have my baby, and we were both happy about it. To top it all off, I was being faithful. For once, I didn't constantly feel like I was looking over my shoulder. The feelings of guilt and shame were put aside, and I enjoyed being a husband.

As the saying goes, I arrived. This feeling of bliss lasted well until my son was five-months-old. Everything was great in our relationship. There was no arguing or fighting. We enjoyed the same type of things in life and had a cool blended family. She got pregnant a second time, and suddenly we were on the pregnancy journey again. It was drama-free and exhilarating. I couldn't have been happier, and I think no one could have been happier for us. What more could I ask for? In time, I fell back into my path of destruction. I cheated with a good friend of the family within a year of marriage.

We hung out with this friend and her husband often. They were our go-to couple for nights out, so it was normal for us to invite each other over for dinner. I don't know how it happened. Once we had some alone time together, I felt the same excitement for her that I felt for my wife. They were both fun-loving, strong women; however, there was something charming and alluring about this friend of ours. I got lucky with her in more ways than one. She had a lot to lose. Her husband was wealthy and smart, and she was under a prenuptial agreement with extensive fidelity clauses. We were extremely careful; she more so than I.

As we got closer and more involved, we saw each other more frequently. Sometimes, we took unnecessary risks. Once, a mutual friend showed up at one of our meeting locations. Luckily, we could play the slip-up off, saying that our spouses were both running late. We heard no rumors, and nothing seemed to have gotten out. To not cause any harm or bring suspicion upon ourselves, we backed away from our relationship. She reiterated she had too much to lose, and I didn't want to involve myself in this cycle again.

I did well for about nine months until the same thing happened again with a different friend. It became standard procedure. We gained friends, usually people we partied with, dined with, or just hung out with. I would then sleep with those friends. Cheating became as second-nature as holding the door for someone behind me. I became numb to unnecessary emotions. Gone were the days I thought pleasing a woman and having her please me meant we were in love and destined to spend our lives together. I developed the ability to have sex with my wife, meet someone at a hotel a couple of hours later, and then set up a meeting later in that day with yet another. Cheating became easy. Granted, I was in no real danger of being found out—my affairs were never suspected nor revealed—but I made sure my tracks were covered.

Even though this was the pattern I worked within, I could not understand how or why I was continuing to sleep with my wife's friends and my friends' wives. Deep down, I knew I was better than this. Guilt visited me often, but I couldn't stop. I was trying to satisfy a craving that came from an unknown place inside of me. I was embodying Romans 7:19-20 which reads, "For the good that I want, I do not do, but I practice the very evil that I do not want. But if I am doing the very thing I do not want, I am no longer the one doing it, but sin which dwells in me." *

As I watched the relationships around me crumble, I often questioned myself about what would happen if anyone found out about my numerous affairs. Despite the things I did, I loved my wife and children. I didn't want to be away from my children. In efforts to be more careful with my affairs, I displayed no affection towards them. It became a priority to treat them in the same manner I did before I had sex with them.

My mother and sisters taught me how to treat women, and I used it to my advantage. I piqued the interest of women, and they gravitated towards me in response. Again, this attention was not unwelcomed; I couldn't let the attention jeopardize the life I'd built.

# CHAPTER SEVEN

# HOW FAITH BEGAN TO FRAME MY FUTURE

Things were calm within my marriage, and everything was going well. My boys were good. I now had custody of my daughter. All of my children were in one place. Money was rolling in. I could comfortably take care of them and my wife. I was on top. It was during this time that Hurricane Katrina hit Louisiana. While watching the weather forecasts, we decided to evacuate. I had an uncle in Leavenworth, Kansas and planned to stay with him. His house was large, so there were two spare bedrooms. Since there were three children, my wife and I took the smaller of the two rooms so they could have more room.

Towards the end of our stay, my uncle asked me what my purpose here was on earth. I didn't know how to answer the question as it was one I never considered. At that time, I was making over $200,000 per year and felt I could compete with him financially, if that was his reason for asking the question.

After some thought, I told him my purpose was to make a lot of money. He was well-educated, a high-ranked officer in the military, and financially stable for some time. This put pressure on me to answer the question correctly. He shook his head furiously saying, "No. That is what you do, but what is your purpose?" Feeling slightly embarrassed, I wasn't sure. I walked with him into the living area where my boys were playing video games. My uncle pointed to them and asked me what I was doing about my salvation. He told me to consider it because everything I did from this point on would directly affect them and my daughter. I thought, Whoa, where is this coming from? I looked at him puzzled because his statement startled me. This wasn't coming from my uncle who preached to me about attending church for God-knows-how-long. This was coming from a different uncle who was gone most of my adult life.

He was now something else, what I couldn't say. But he must have sensed something in me that loved those children and would have done anything for them. I pondered his statements as he rummaged around a bookshelf, the smell of dust invading the air.

Finally, he found the book he was looking for. "Here," he said in his gruff, authoritative voice while placing the book in my hands. "I want you to read this." I looked down at the book: Rick Warren's, A Purpose Driven Life. I felt a frown forming. I hated reading. I couldn't remember the last time I willingly picked up a book, but I knew it had probably been years.

"I'm not saying you have to like it, but I am suggesting you read it." He stared me down. "And when you're done, I want to know what you think about it." I nodded slowly. "Thank you, sir," I said, "I'll read it."

My uncle went back to his seat, and I took the book to my room. I looked at the cover. A pencil-shaded green tree with the title written in large font. The word life stood out, as it was the only word written in cursive. Also, it was the only word written in the same ugly, purple font as the border of the cover art. Purple and pastel yellow. The color scheme did not interest me. Why this book? I asked myself as I turned it over.

On the back were paragraphs in relatively small print. I didn't bother to read them. I rolled my eyes and checked to see how many pages there were. The three-digit page number began with a 3, which made me toss the book on the bed and exit the room. I didn't want to break a promise I just made and especially not to my uncle. Serious doubts crossed my mind whether I wanted to subject myself to the torture that book surely contained. Reading the book was not my desire. We left my uncle's house the next day.

The storm was over, and it was safe to fly back to Houston and survey the damage. We were lucky. Our house was only missing a few shingles, and there were a few stray branches here and there in the yard. Not all of my neighbors were as lucky. Some of them ended up paying over $20,000 in damages. My mind wandered to the book my uncle gave me the day before, and I couldn't help but wonder if this was some sign. Why were we spared the brunt of the storm while others had not? Over the last few years, I was lucky for all intents and purposes. Was this just more evidence of my good fortune? I couldn't think of a satisfactory answer to these questions but decided that if this was in fact proof of my luck, I was more than ok with it.

The remainder of the day was spent repairing the minimal amounts of damage and unpacking. I grudgingly began reading the book the next day. I still didn't know what the book was about, as I hadn't bothered to revisit the back cover. However, I definitely wanted to keep my word to my uncle. There was an uneasy feeling, like my uncle was warning me of some unforetold danger only he could see. I wanted to be armed with every weapon possible to ensure the well-being of my children wouldn't be threatened. Reading three-hundred-plus pages in a night, or even in a week was impossible. Setting a goal to read at least a chapter a day was best for me.

**God's House**

Day after day, I read this book about purpose. On the first Sunday back in Houston, I went to a church that a friend of mine told me about for some time. She spoke highly of her pastor and of his sermons.

Before my first son was born, I paid a short visit to the church, but only because she would be there. This was the same friend I was connected to when I first got married. This time was different because I would not see her or any other lady friends. I was going for a different reason entirely, one that churchgoers would say was the right reason.

My church experience was all about me wanting to be a better father, not necessarily about the addiction. During the process of becoming a better father, it opened my mind to other areas I needed to work on. Being a good father was the most important thing and the best contribution I could make in the world. It shifted my attention to something more than myself, the something greater than my addiction.

Week after week, I went to this church and found it rather interesting. Many of the practices were foreign to me. Ironically, I wasn't raised in church. It was a charismatic,

Bible-based church, which was what I needed. Every Sunday, people were dancing, falling out, screaming, and crying. The pastor was very meticulous. With a methodical approach, his intelligence rang as surreal. She did not lie when she said he was captivating. I fell deeper into these messages and looked forward to being in attendance each week.

The members were friendly and accepted me without question. They had no clue who I was or what I was about. For once, it didn't seem to matter. The spirit everyone talked about finally crept upon me. I was uncertain what spirit it was. Whatever it was, it drove me to stand up when they asked who among the crowd wished to dedicate their lives to Jesus. I wanted to be saved and a true member of the church. The music surrounded me, and people cheered and clapped. There was a noise that rivaled the sound of a hotly contested ball game. I would give my life to the Lord.

Things were not perfect, and I was still cheating. Even though I went to church regularly, I still met up with one of my newest lovers. We went to our usual spot to do our usual thing. I told her I volunteered to be saved. She asked when, and I told her yesterday at church. A mass of jumbled emotions crossed her face, but she simply said now things would change. I asked her what she meant, but she didn't elaborate. Being saved would be a good thing, and I tried to make her see that. I could be faithful, and she and her husband could strengthen their relationship. We tried to break it off with each other several times, but the cycle we were caught in was too intoxicating. I was confused why this was still happening.

I was finding out the new creature I thought I would become wasn't new. In fact, he looked a lot like the old me, whom I had been trying to eradicate. Worried that I would be an inherently bad person doomed to spend an eternity in Hell, I asked an elder what was wrong with me. He told me this was normal, saying the wicked one came with tests to make me doubt my salvation. He warned me to disregard these attempts because he could not stop me from walking out my purpose. There was that word again, purpose. The same word from the book I finished reading a few months back. I decided to stop seeing her. I lost count of the number of times I failed. After about a month, it was time for the baptism. I had never been baptized, so I was excited. This would help me resolve my problem.

**Baptism**

My baptism was scheduled for the same weekend as my cousin's wedding. Refusing to miss either, I booked my itinerary accordingly. The baptism was scheduled for one o'clock on that Sunday, and my flight would land at noon. My wife and I were flying from the wedding in Maryland. We just experienced the matrimony of two people and were extremely excited for them. I remember tugging at my clothes the entire time I was on the plane, repeatedly adjusting myself and hoping the plane would arrive on time. It was just a few minutes off schedule, but those extra few minutes threw me into a slight panic.

Grabbing my things as quickly as I could, I rushed to my car. I nearly ran into a couple of people in the process. By the grace of God, I made it there right on time. I took my spot behind the last person in line, looking out at the crowd of members. My grandparents and uncles supported me on my new journey. The pastor took my hand and asked me a couple of questions. After I answered them, he said something about the Father, the Son, and The Holy Ghost and dipped me backwards into the freezing water. I came up, both hands in the air, and yelled Yes. Everyone was cheering and clapping, but I was in my own world.

At that moment, I realized I had the opportunity to be that new person everyone told me about. The day had finally come, and all my worries were over. I had done it. Monday morning came and alerted me that the baptism did not do the trick. No matter how much screaming and cheering it had brought out of us the day before, I seemed to be the same person.

A couple of weeks prior, I broke it off with my love interest. We ended up reconnecting, meeting at our usual spot and doing our usual thing. It was a mystery why the baptism didn't work. Once again, I met my lover at the hotel again. We did everything we normally did. Although I enjoyed it, I was not as excited about it. Self-control was lacking in my life. Even seeking God did not do the trick. I scheduled our meetings so they were less frequent. She sensed something was different, but I assured her it was not her fault. Internal battles were present within both of us since we both cheated on our spouses, however I knew her issues weren't as deep as mine. Both of us were married to other people, so we couldn't be together. I had been down that road before and wasn't willing to go down it again. This time, I wanted to do right. Her husband was my homeboy, and my wife was her friend. There was no way this could work.

Everything urged me to do right by the people I loved. I began to wean myself off her. Others came along, mostly old flames who served many purposes in the past, wanting to reconnect with me. I couldn't help but to indulge in them. These were the ones I knew I could get away with seeing. I already experienced dealing with them. The allure of easy opportunities, high gains and low risks was too much for me to pass up. In some way, it felt like I adopted a new sin, low-stakes gambling. The more I earned, the greedier I became.

My relationship with the pastor grew as I participated in the ministry. Rich, educational and inspirational messages were being fed to me every week. There was a lack of comfortability when it came to discussing my issues with the pastor, but I found a friend and confidant in his son. I told him about my struggles and affairs. Being offered words of advice and spiritual counseling helped me become accountable for my actions. I told him how I used to drink, cuss, lie, and even steal. Sometimes it felt like God took away those sins after the baptism, yet he left me with the worst one of all. I asked him why he wouldn't take away that sin too or at least give me an easier one to deal with. My friend simply said that my desire to sin would keep me dependent on God. It would make me seek His healing. This was my cross to bear.

With the relationship being over with my lover, here was the perfect time to be right. It was just me and my wife. I was saved, baptized, and regularly attending church. My wife visited a few times; however, she did not attend as much as I did. This was a burden, but I needed this to get on the right track. So, I kept going to church because I could not afford to be sidetracked. Little did I know this great place would become my biggest challenge.

Church was one of the most enticing places for my type. There were friendly women everywhere I looked. Greeting at the door, ushering into the sanctuary, singing in the choir—they outnumbered the men five to one by my count. This was amazing for the old me. However, I wanted the new me to win this time. How would I be able to do this with temptation at every turn? This was the equivalent to an alcoholic sitting in a liquor store or a drug addict who just won the lottery.

Since I had not been in church before but knew church people were good and were doing the right thing, I felt ok. Until I asked one of them to do some work for me. Then it happened; we were engaging in sex. How could this be happening with a church girl? It seemed to be easier with her than the others I had been with before being introduced to church. This whole new life, new creature thing was confusing. My behavior continued. I was at the right place, trying to do the right things, engaging with the right people, and somehow still did the wrong things.

# CHAPTER EIGHT

# BREAKING THE SILENCE

While I understand change is a process that takes time, understanding did not keep me from being disturbed. I often wondered if I was missing something. I couldn't help but ask myself why this wasn't getting better or going away altogether. Why wasn't I good enough to be one of those that God worked for? Was I underqualified? I was the ministry leader. I should have been qualified for some healing too, right? What did those saved, happy people at the front of the church have inside of them that I lacked? And how could I get what they had, or could I? All I could do was pray about it and hope that God send me a sign.

I felt like a coward, like I needed to man up. What I presented to the world was not a true representation of where I was in my life. I wanted to deal with my truth even if I couldn't handle it on my own.

43

**My Sign**

One Sunday morning, the pastor made a comment that woke me up. He said, "While salvation is instantaneous, deliverance is a process." That was the answer I was waiting for. This whole time I sought instantaneous deliverance, but that's why I was unsuccessful. I did not know what the process was. Being curious about what I needed to do to get the process to come to fruition, I scheduled a meeting with the pastor for the following week. I was confident that expressing my situation to him would guide me and help me be a better person. He was my spiritual father. Our relationship was concrete enough for me to trust him. Constantly fearing judgment caused me to want to figure things out for myself. Never had I asked for this kind of help before; this was huge for me.

**Asking for Help**

We visited for about an hour. Initially, I did all the talking. I told my pastor I was weak. No one had any idea how long this was going on. After I went through my whole history, I begged him to help me find answers because I wanted to be better. I didn't want to be this person anymore. He looked at me more sternly than I was used to but also paternally. He leaned back in his chair, sighing, and folding his hands across his belly. "Drew," he said. "Your issue is more than a surface issue. You have a lot of deep-rooted issues you need to deal with." While I knew this to be true, it was hard for me to hear it from someone else, especially someone I respected so much. He referred me to a counselor who specialized in sexual disorders. Before I walked out of the door, I set my appointment.

## Professional Help

I was nervous as I drove to meet my counselor for the first time. My only previous encounter with a counselor was the one at my high school. Even still, I never visited with her, just saw her in passing. As I sat in his office and waited to be seen, I prayed. I told God I wanted to be better, and I would do whatever I needed to do to get better. This burden was one I could no longer bear, so I was open to any changes I had to make.

I arrived at the counselor's office. The waiting period was surprisingly long even though I was one of few patients there. I read the six inspirational posters hanging in the small office about 90 times. My nervous energy grew and fed my insecurities. I didn't know what to expect. Sitting in a waiting room to see a counselor about my addiction to sex when I never saw myself as a sex addict was beyond uncomfortable. I was mortified. As I considered rescheduling, the counselor entered before I could.

Our session was concise and direct. He asked me why I was there, so I explained to him the position I was in for as long as I could remember. From there, I elaborated on how it made me feel. I told him I feared I would ruin my marriage and then rattled off even more fears associated with divorce. My immediate goal was to find the best and fastest way to quit so I could maintain my relationship with my wife. My counselor stopped me with a statement that changed my perspective. He said, "Mr. Landry, I am not a marriage counselor. I am not here to save your marriage or prevent you from experiencing another divorce. If you want to save your marriage, you will need to find someone else to help you. I am here only to help you get better. If you want to get better for yourself, I can help you with that. I'll instruct you. If you follow my instructions, you will get better."

He shared success stories about his clients. The computer screen was turned towards me. Outlined was his "12-Step Process to Recovery", along with some statistics. I was encouraged to go through this with my wife. This was important to my recovery because I needed to be held accountable by myself and those around me.

Instantly, I dreaded telling my wife because she had no clue I was cheating. I almost argued, but I remembered I told God I would do whatever He said. My wife knew I was going to a counselor already, but she didn't know the reasoning. As we were closing the session, he asked me if I wanted to save my marriage or if I wanted to get better. I told him that more than anything I wanted to be a better person. He went over my first steps one more time then reiterated that I needed to go home and tell my wife everything and anything she wanted to know. I asked what I should do if she asked for names, but he raised his hand and told me once again that I needed to tell her everything. She needed to have all the information so she could go through the steps with me.

After I completed my homework, I was to meet him again the next week so we could discuss the outcomes and tweak our approaches for the successive steps. Regret about coming crept upon me, but I agreed I would do my best if it would help me in the long run. I was more worried when I left than I was when I arrived at the office. My heart was pounding, and it felt like the neckline of my shirt was suffocating me. I was hot and sweaty. Once I got into the car, I turned the AC on full blast. As the cold air hit me in the face, I gripped the steering wheel.

# CHAPTER NINE

# CONFESSION

I was certain my wife would ask for names. Most of these people were close friends of ours, so I couldn't give their names to her. I thought about lying and making up names. It wouldn't matter if the names were real or not. I still cheated, right? I knew I was wrong. Overcoming this was my desire more than anything. Becoming a better person was more important than saving my marriage. What would stop me from telling her their names?

In my heart, I prayed that I didn't have to reveal the identities of my lovers. If I were in her shoes, the names would be the first thing I'd ask for. Even though I didn't want to do it, I had to. The counselor ended our session by telling me that if I could not complete these steps, to not bother returning. If I was not willing to put in the work, he would not waste his time trying to help me. I made a promise to God I would do it because I knew that if I made a promise to God, I would keep it.

I looked at the icebreaker DVD the counselor gave me to help break the news to her. The DVD was about coping with sexual addiction and telling your loved ones. I'm not sure how things took such a drastic turn. Here I was sitting in my car diagnosed with Compulsive Sexual Disorder and facing the prospect of ruining my marriage with this news. The whole thing was strange. Until this point, I thought people could only be classified as addicts if they had problems with drugs, alcohol, or gambling—not sex. But again, I was wrong. Thoughts raced through my head as I drove.

After running a red light and nearly causing an accident, I pulled over in a Dollar Store parking lot. Because of this counselor's insanity, I had no idea what I should do. He couldn't know what he was talking about or the consequences that following his guidance would have for me. I had an ideal marriage to a beautiful woman who never gave me any trouble. She was easy to live with, took good care of not only our children together but also my daughter, and was unaware of my infidelity. Why did I have to tell her? Couldn't I let this die and move forward from here? I had no one else to turn to, so I called my pastor, who by this time referred to me as son. I told him about the session and asked him if I should tell her. He told me, "Of course. She had the right to know since so many other people did." This was not what I wanted to hear. There were many people I could call to tell me don't risk it, but those voices would just stand in the way of me doing what I know I needed to do. I refused to take the easy way out. I sighed and checked both ways before driving back onto the road. I knew what I had to do, but I didn't feel like I was strong enough to do it.

## Telling Wasn't Easy

When I made it to the house, she was in the kitchen. She asked how the meeting went, and I shouted back to her from the living room that it went well. I made my way to the bedroom, dressed down, and continued my day as if nothing had happened. We later ate dinner with the children and then helped them prepare for bed. By now I decided to tell her, but I was still struggling with how to do so. Luckily, I still had the DVD. When we were in bed, I leaned over and told her the therapist gave me a DVD to watch with her. She smiled and said, "Yeah, definitely." All the anxiety I was fighting all day intensified.

She was a sweet woman. I didn't want to hurt her, but I wanted to get this over with. I popped the DVD into the player, and we watched it. After a few minutes, confusion washed over her face. "What is this about?" she asked. I sighed, grabbed the remote and shut off the TV. The couple shown looked a lot happier than my wife and I would be. "I went to see a therapist because I have a problem," I said. "Okay," she said, dragging out the last syllable. "What kind of problem?" Unsure of how to say it, I ended up bluntly telling her I was a sex addict and had been cheating on her.

Bracing myself, I pulled away from her because I expected her to slap me, attack me, or something. She did none of the above. Her gloomy eyes lowered towards the sheets as she sat across from me. Tears formed in her eyes, causing me to look away because she did not cry often. As I expected, she asked who I cheated with. I still wasn't prepared for the question and did not want to answer it. My promise to God and my counselor came to mind. One after the other, names spewed from my mouth. When I was finally done with the list of names, I dared to look back at her.

Every trace of sadness disappeared from her face; it was replaced with a look of utter serenity. "Ok then," she said. Pulling the covers around her, she turned facing the opposite direction. I wanted to speak, but I didn't know what I could say, so I swallowed the lump in my throat and followed her motion. She fell asleep first. I could not; her cool response frightened me.

## The Beginning of the End

Little conversation occurred the next morning. Her tone was the same. Even though she looked like she had it all together, I could sense she didn't. I made myself as scarce as possible, not wanting to bring forth whatever wrath she held beneath the surface. Phone calls to the people I told my wife about occupied most of my time. At least they would have forewarning and could prepare themselves accordingly; I would have wanted the same courtesy from them if the roles were reversed. It was important to inform them that my wife knew the whole story now. Out of respect for her, there was no need for me to communicate with them anymore. I made it clear I wanted to do the right thing and would be solely focused on repairing the damage done to my marriage. They all understood as they now had issues of their own to confront.

As promised, I attended my session with my therapist the next week. We discussed the interactions I had with my wife since the big reveal, and he asked if she was onboard with my recovery. Since I didn't have the nerve to ask her outright, I wasn't entirely sure. Although I didn't expect her to attend any sessions with me, I assumed she would support me through my recovery. Saying the next few weeks were strained would be an understatement, but it seemed as though we were making progress. Some of her tenderness was returning, and I felt some fire inside of her was calming down.

Other than my hopefulness, I had no real basis for these assumptions. I was adamant things would improve. Every day I made steps towards doing right by her. As long as she could see that, things would be ok.

My relationship with my wife became more strained; a great distance grew between us. It happened gradually. Once we noticed it, it was too late. I came home from work one day to find her packing her clothes. Most of her things were together, separated in little piles around the room. I was confused as to what was happening and why it was happening now. I was coping with my lifelong issue and hadn't cheated since the night I confessed to her. My spiritual life was great. But even still, I was losing my wife and my kids. This was not the storybook ending I thought I would get. Everything I worked to save was fading.

Whether it was because of embarrassment, hurt or betrayal, she decided she was leaving. It was clear she would no longer be in the same house with me. I tried to talk her out of it but to no avail. The doorbell rang. I watched as the movers removed things, item by item. The hardest part of watching was the fact this was her family; the same people who saw us as a great couple and were genuinely happy for us when we got married.

Reality sunk in. This right move, to recognize that deliverance is a process, caused me a great loss. The day she officially left, her cousin said, "Drew, it was bold of you to tell her everything. I would have never done that." I was hurt but told him I wanted to do the right thing. Before he left, he shook my hand and said he respected me for my courage. I looked at the car which she was already firmly seated in. Right then and there, I told him I wholeheartedly believed God would bring my wife back to me. I kept the house, and she moved in with her mother. The kids stayed with me until they finished out the school year. It was bittersweet, as I still had the most important people, my kids, but I had to live without my wife.

By the time summer came, we were on sharing terms. Our responsibilities were split down the middle. Spending nine years together helped us be civil. Plus, she wasn't much of a fighter. Even when I was belligerent, she remained calm and collected. We had a few heated encounters, primarily because I was fighting to get her to hold on to what I destroyed. We eventually divorced, and I was left with nothing.

## More Loss

To make matters worse, my finances plummeted. My house went up for foreclosure, my cars were repossessed, and I had no family to lean on. I was at the lowest place I could ever remember being in. I was homeless, sleeping in the one car I left at our friend's house when they were generous enough to let me. I even slept in my storage building a few times. The wheels fell off, but somewhere was still better than nowhere.

I believed God would honor my decision to do the right thing. After all, I was under the direction of wise counsel. It was a struggle, but I kept pushing. Growing in the knowledge of God and the Word, I knew He would not allow me to give up the fight. I chose not to continue with therapy; I wanted God to prove Himself to me, so I became fully dependent on Him. No longer did I need the DVDs given to me during the sessions. I traded those tools for the whole armor of God, of which was application of the Word. Revelations 12:11 (NKJV) was one of the Bible verses that helped me. It says, "And they overcame him by the blood of the Lamb and by the word of their testimony..." I took these words to heart, and they are part of the reason I am so adamant about encouraging you to share your testimony and talk about the addiction no one has.

Once I started living by these words, things turned around for me. I kept faith He would give my wife back. Consistently working on being a better man, He rewarded me with her. We eventually rekindled and remarried for a short time. The fidelity was there, however the mounting pressure to keep it together was not bearable for her. She left, and we divorced again. I'm proud to say I overcame the desire to cheat.

# CHAPTER TEN

# I WON'T GO BACK

Throughout my entire childhood and adulthood, I carried this burden alone. Like many sex addicts, I suffered in private. As a man, it felt necessary to deal with my problems on my own. I didn't talk about them with anyone because I thought it was normal. Sex was always on my mind. All day, every day. Like most sex addicts, I didn't realize this was a compulsion.

I blame those who introduced me to sex prematurely. Because of their actions, I used sex to cover up my inability to be intimate. It would be years before I sought treatment. I lost my wife, my kids, and my finances plummeted. I was bankrupt both literally and figuratively.

My conscious was numb. Sexual pleasure was more important than reason until the act was over. It was the louder voice. I wanted no one to get hurt, but harming people emotionally came with the territory.

I became angry with God after I confessed. Things didn't turn out the way I hoped for even though I believed I was doing the right thing. In my heart, I believed God failed me when I lost everything. Although I expected the consequences of what I did wrong, I was angry with God because I didn't experience the blessings connected to what I did right. Over time, I understood that loss was associated with me gaining a relationship with God. That was the blessing.

Once I realized my problem and took an active role in overcoming it through Christ, things turned around for me. I still suffered. There were many casualties, but sometimes you have to lose in order to gain.

**Real Change**

Something has to compel you to change. You will not be successful in overcoming sexual addiction if you continue to live in the same cycle. Work on self-control. It may seem difficult since it requires the mental capacity and desire to change. You must believe your future, your family, and your legacy are worth it. Never become satisfied with the progress you've made. Be proud of your successes, but don't get complacent. Would I consider myself successful? In ways, yes. However, I still struggle every day and realize this is a process. Deliverance is a process. Sin will keep you dependent upon God only if you desire to please Him. Although I'm proud of the progress I've made, I know there's more work to be done.

My goal is to help. Some studies estimate that the number of people battling sex addiction is significantly higher than what we think. People go untreated. Like me, they may be unaware they have a diagnosable problem. They might feel that something is off, but are too embarrassed to seek help. There is no shame in wanting to better yourself or in telling your story. The more we talk about sex addiction, the more it will help others. One thing that prompted me to write this book is that there's no real conversation around this.

In the old church, there was a thing called testimony service. People would get up and say they were alcoholics, drug abusers, prostitutes, crooks and other things, however God delivered them. I never heard of anyone saying I am a sex addict. I believe sex addiction to be one of the most difficult addictions to overcome because no one is talking about it, and sex is natural. It's in God's plan for mankind to procreate. It is the perversion of a natural act that causes it to be very difficult to triumph.

I know this is not an easy battle and I do not want to minimize the extreme work required to overcome addiction, but I maintain my position on the power of testimony. The words uttered in Revelation 12:11 (NKJV) reigns true. It reads, "And they overcame him by the blood of the Lamb and by the word of their testimony, and they did not love their lives to death." I will not say it is the only way, but I believe it to be the most effective for me.

# CHAPTER ELEVEN

# A SECOND CHANCE AT LIFE AND LOVE

Eventually, I married a beautiful, saved, young woman who loved Jesus as much as I do. We pray, worship, and serve in ministry together. This is the reward God had in store for me. While I was struggling with the loss of my ex-wife, I prayed to God to give her back. My faith is what I believe allowed us to reconnect for a brief period. My relationship with God became so intense that my prayer changed from getting back together to God, I want someone who loves me like you do. He did both. God not only gave me the desires of my heart, he also helped place me in a position of loving only one woman. He continues to equip me with the tools to be effective in my struggles. While I don't want to lose everything again, the thing I cannot afford to lose is GOD.

When I was at my lowest, I realized the power that came with walking with God. While the times were rough, the walk with God became more important than the fear of losing things. This level of realization came through loss, so I urge people to find the one thing that is more important than their addiction. Think about how you would feel if you woke up in the morning and didn't have access to that thing. Is your addiction worth that? If you can honestly say it isn't, what steps can you take right now to change your behavior?

# CHAPTER TWELVE

# WHAT I UNDERSTAND NOW

Looking back on life has a way of revealing truth like nothing else. Here are a few lessons I learned about myself once I took the time to reflect.

**Lesson 1**

Men are not known for being open and sharing, and I found this often hinders us from overcoming our struggles. We have trouble expressing how we feel. If you throw in confusion, disappointment, and violation, we're at a loss for words.

Being able to express our feelings plays a role in the cleansing we need to change. We have to deal with our stuff to get over our stuff. It helps in the process of emerging from the shadows of our pain. Confronting our issues and talking about how we've been violated, abandoned, or mishandled from an early age helps us to regain our personal power.

This was true for me. I spent years battling internal conflict before I had the courage to ask for help.

**Lesson 2**

Men are visual creatures, and it's hard to fight an innate behavior. Today, I continue to be active in the church. As mentioned, lust within the church is everywhere. Women make up a large majority of a church's membership. For a sex addict, it can be a place that feeds the addiction. Opportunities are abundant. Here, it is best to remember the teachings of the Lord and to know the wicked one capitalizes on our weaknesses. Even Jesus was tested, and we are not exempt from temptation either. But we have to choose to believe in the power of God.

**Lesson 3**

Men have a tendency to be prideful and maybe even stubborn. We want to do things on our own and often can't, but need to be comfortable in order to receive help. We can be ego-driven and find it difficult presenting our issues.

**Lesson 4**

Men can appear closed off or withdrawn. If we are not comfortable or safe, we won't express ourselves. We don't share because we don't feel safe to share. We often fear judgment and embarrassment. This is one reason I remained silent for so long.

**Lesson 5**

Men struggle with change, particularly changing what we believe and the way we think. I knew I needed to change and wanted to change. It was difficult understanding how change would show up in my life or the tools to make it happen. We often need a shift, but need to know where to shift to.

**Lesson 6**

Men must learn how to be vulnerable. This was one of the hardest things for me to overcome. I viewed vulnerability as a sign of weakness instead of strength; but learned the opposite was true. I learned vulnerability in the right setting was a demonstration of strength.

**Lesson 7**

Men struggle with wearing masks. For me, I grew complacent because I served in ministry while hiding behind a mask. I couldn't afford to be found out, looked down upon, or shamed. The real me and my issues had to be confronted. In the process, I also realized transition can take place without being messy. I'm thankful for the men God placed in my life to guide me through it without exploiting me or my family.

## Lesson 8

We fear seeking because we fear what we may find. This was true for me. Once I fully knew I had a serious problem, the thought of seeking help frightened me initially. I feared what it would require of me, and I was afraid of failing. In time, I learned that was just the lie I was telling myself.

Help is available, whether by pastoral care or professional counseling. I will not say a three-step program or twelve-step program is more effective but can say the method I used worked for me. It involved admission, confession/testimony, accountability and seeking professional help. These were invaluable in the process of my overcoming addiction.

# AUTHOR'S NOTE

Dear Reader,

Throughout this text you have journeyed with me as I shared my story of overcoming sex addiction. During this journey, I have been candid about my relationship with my Lord and Savior, Jesus Christ. If you already have a relationship with Jesus Christ, that's awesome. I pray that you continue to grow in your faith. However, if you do not have a relationship with Jesus Christ and would like Him to be your Lord and Savior, I invite you to pray this prayer out loud:

# PRAYER OF SALVATION

Dear God, I need You. I am calling out to You. I'm tired of doing things my way. Help me to start doing things Your way. I invite You into my life to be my Lord and Savior. Fill the emptiness in me with your Holy Spirit and make me whole. Lord, help me to trust You. Help me to love You. Help me to live for You. Help me to understand Your grace, Your mercy and Your peace.

Thank you for loving me, Lord. I love You, too.

In Jesus' name, Amen!

Name: _____

Date: _____

If this was your first time praying this prayer, or if you simply prayed the prayer to reaffirm your faith in Jesus, this is the first step to changing your life forever. I encourage you to find a church and Christian community! This journey isn't meant to be traveled alone. Congratulations and thank you for taking this journey with me.

Thanks,
*Andrew J. Landry*

# REFLECTION

What is greater than your addiction?

What is the one thing you cannot live without (that is not your addiction)?

What is your addiction?

When did you first recognize the issue?

What characteristics lead you to see you have/had an issue?

What reckless behaviors do you display?

What is your biggest fear with those behaviors?

What trigger/actions keep leading you to the same place?

How can you redirect those triggers?

What do you use to rationalize your destructive behavior?

Why do you see this as a problem?

Name the people you have to hold you accountable

Why did you choose these particular people?

What do you do when you relapse?

How do you respond to those who should be happy for you but are not?

How do you fight off the thoughts that make improper behavior appealing?

What do you do when your safe place becomes a breeding place for your demise?

What professional and/or spiritual help have you reached out for?

What direction was given, and are you following it?

How much are you willing to risk to get better?

What can you do to trust the process instead of focusing on the possibility of loss?

Are you willing to take the first step today? How?

Once you have gotten to a better state, are you willing to share your story? Who are you willing to share your story with?

# RESOURCES

**Sex Addiction**
Sex Addicts Anonymous (SAA):
1-800-477-8191
https://saa-recovery.org

**SAMHSA's National Helpline**
(800) 662-HELP (4357)
https://www.samhsa.gov/find-help/national-helpline

**All Crisis**
Crisis Call Center
800-273-8255 or text ANSWER to 839863
http://crisiscallcenter.org/crisisservices.html

**National Hopeline Network**
800-SUICIDE (784-2433); 800-442-HOPE (4673)
http://www.hopeline.com

**Alcoholism**
Alcoholics Anonymous
(212) 870-3400
http://www.aa.org

**Drug Abuse**
Narcotics Anonymous
(818) 773-9999
https://www.na.org

**Mental Health**
National Mental Health Association Hotline
1-800-273-TALK (8255)
http://www.nmha.org

**Sexual Assault**
National Sexual Assault Hotline
1-800-656-4673 [24/7 hotline]
https://rainn.org

**Suicide**
National Suicide Prevention Lifeline
1-800-273-TALK (8255) [24/7 hotline]; 1-888-628-9454
(Spanish)
http://www.suicidepreventionlifeline.org

# REFERENCES

Fong, Timothy W., (Nov 2006). "Understanding and Managing Compulsive Sexual Behaviors." *Psychiatry (Edgmont)*. Retrieved from: https://www.ncbi.nlm.nih.gov/pmc/articles/PMC2945841/

Szalavitz, Maia, (Oct 2012). "Study Supports Sex Addiction as a Diagnosis-Worthy Disorder." *Time Magazine*. Retrieved from: http://healthland.time.com/2012/10/24/study-supports-sex-addiction-as-a-diagnosis-worthy-disorder/

Wery, Aline; Vogelaere, Kim; Challet-Bouju, Gaelle; Poudat, Francios-Xavier; Caillon, Julie; Lever, Delphine; Billieux, Joel; Grall-Bronnec, Marie. (Dec 2016). "Characteristics of self-identified sexual addicts in a behavioral outpatient clinic." *Journal of Behavioral Addiction*. Retrieved from: https://www.ncbi.nlm.nih.gov/pmc/articles/PMC5370367/

Singh, Mannat Mohanjeet; Parsekar, Shradha S.; Nair, Sreekumaran N. (Oct-Dec 2014). "An Epidemiological Overview of Child Sexual Abuse." *Journal of Family Medicine*. Retrieved from: https://www.ncbi.nlm.nih.gov/pmc/articles/PMC4311357/